DRAGON PARADE
A CHINESE NEW YEAR STORY

by Steven A. Chin

Alex Haley, General Editor

Illustrations by Mou-Sien Tseng

RSVP
RAINTREE
STECK-VAUGHN
PUBLISHERS
The Steck-Vaughn Company

Austin, Texas

This book is dedicated to my grandparents,
Chun K. Chow and Ivy, who left Toishan, China,
to build a new life in America.

Published by Steck-Vaughn Company.

Text, illustrations, and cover art copyright © 1993 by Dialogue Systems, Inc., 627 Broadway, New York , New York 10012.
All rights reserved.

Cover art by Mou-Sien Tseng

Printed in China

16 0940 11
4500290262

Library of Congress Cataloging-in-Publication Data

Chin, Steven A., 1959–
    Dragon Parade: a Chinese New Year story / author, Steven A. Chin; illustrator, Mou-Sien Tseng.
        p. cm.—(Stories of America)
    ISBN 0-8114-7215-9 (hardcover).—ISBN 0-8114-8055-0 (softcover)
    1. New Year—California—Chinatown (San Francisco)—History—Juvenile literature. 2. Chinatown (San Francisco, Calif.)—Social life and customs—Juvenile literature. 3. Chinese Americans—California—Chinatown (San Francisco)—Social life and customs. I. Tseng, Mou-Sien. II. Title. III. Series.
GT4905.C4B 1993
394.2'683—dc20

92–18079
CIP
AC

ISBN-10: 0-8114-7215-9(Hardcover)
ISBN-13: 978-0-8114-7215-9
ISBN-10: 0-8114-8055-0(Softcover)
ISBN-13: 978-0-8114-8055-0

A Note
from Alex Haley, General Editor

This is a book about new starts. America has given new starts to millions of people from all over the world. It gave one to Norman Ah Sing, whom you will read about in *Dragon Parade*.

The coming of a new year also gives people a chance for a new start. And this is a book about that, too. It is about how Chinese and Chinese Americans begin the New Year—with a celebration and a new start.

Pop! Pop! Pop!

Norman Ah Sing watched the children. They set off long rows of firecrackers.

Gung hay fat choy, he called. I wish you good luck and happiness.

All around Norman's village people said *Gung hay fat choy* to one another. It was the New Year.

In China the New Year began just before springtime. The farmers were about to plant their crops. It was a time of new beginnings—a new year, new crops, new luck and happiness.

Norman was ready for a new beginning, too. But he would not be planting any crops. He was about to begin a great adventure. He was going to the Land of the Golden Mountain!

The Land of the Golden Mountain was America. It lay far, far away from Norman's village. People said the streets there were paved with gold. Everyone could become very rich, they said.

In those days, around 150 years ago, times were hard in China. Many people were poor and hungry. So Chinese men by the hundreds left their villages for the Land of the Golden Mountain. They hoped to make money in America. Then they could help their families.

Norman wanted to help his family, too. He decided to go to the Land of the Golden Mountain.

One day, after the New Year began, Norman said goodbye to his family. He said goodbye to his village. Then he went to the sea where he got on a ship with hundreds of other Chinese men.

It was a new beginning for Norman.

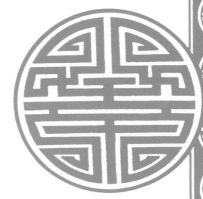

Norman thought the trip would never end. For six weeks huge waves tossed the ship from side to side.

At last the ship landed in San Francisco, California. Norman was very happy. He had arrived in America, the Land of the Golden Mountain.

Then Norman looked around him. He was shocked. Something was wrong. There was not a single street of gold. In fact, there were just a lot of dusty dirt roads. San Francisco was just a very small town.

Where is the gold? Norman asked in Chinatown, where the Chinese people lived.

There is no gold here, they told him. The gold is in the mountains. But it is hard to find. Some people get rich. Most people do not.

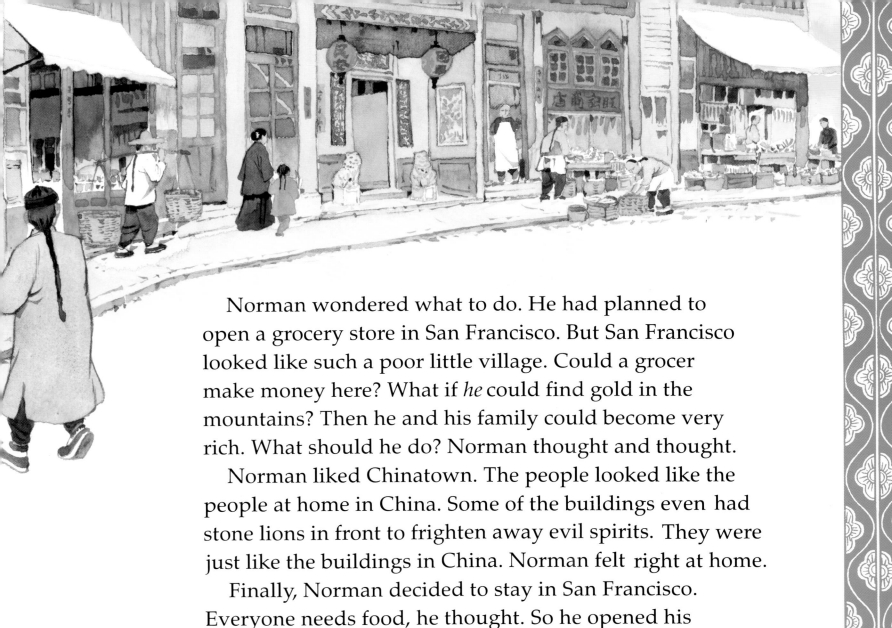

Norman wondered what to do. He had planned to open a grocery store in San Francisco. But San Francisco looked like such a poor little village. Could a grocer make money here? What if *he* could find gold in the mountains? Then he and his family could become very rich. What should he do? Norman thought and thought.

Norman liked Chinatown. The people looked like the people at home in China. Some of the buildings even had stone lions in front to frighten away evil spirits. They were just like the buildings in China. Norman felt right at home.

Finally, Norman decided to stay in San Francisco. Everyone needs food, he thought. So he opened his grocery store.

Every weekend the narrow Chinatown streets were filled with men. They came back from the mountains to visit their friends and to buy groceries. Norman was very busy in his store. Weeks and months passed quickly.

One morning he was surprised. I came to San Francisco almost a year ago, he thought. Soon it will be time to celebrate the New Year again.

Norman knew that the people in Chinatown had a small celebration each year. But in China *everyone* celebrated the New Year. There were parades and parties and wonderful food.

This gave Norman an idea. Why not invite important people from all over San Francisco to celebrate the New Year? Then the people of Chinatown could make new friends.

Norman told everyone in Chinatown about his plan for a big New Year's celebration. They loved his idea.

There was so much to do to get ready for the New Year.

The people of Chinatown had to plan a huge feast
and clean their houses and stores
and hang red scrolls on the windows and doors
and put up paper lanterns

and pay all of the money they owed
and get haircuts
and buy new suits
and go to the temple to pay respects to their
ancestors.
There was so much to do!

Friday was New Year's Eve. Chinese people from all over California had heard about the big celebration. They headed to San Francisco. Even the Chinese miners came down from the mountains.

That night Norman closed his store. It would stay closed for a whole week. The other store owners did the same. They wouldn't have time to work. They would be too busy celebrating!

Everyone in Chinatown had a special dinner that night. Norman and his friends ate New Year's cakes that looked like gold coins. They sang New Year's songs together.

Suddenly a shower of fireworks lit up the black night sky. Chinatown exploded with sound. Cymbals clanged. Horns honked. Firecrackers banged.

The noise was so loud that Norman and his friends could not hear themselves speak. But they were happy. They knew the loud noise would chase away evil spirits.

On New Year's morning, Norman put on his new suit. He knew it was important to do everything just right on this special day. After all, what happens on New Year's Day will happen all year long. So Norman would wear new clothes, think good thoughts, and speak only kind words. Then he would have good luck all year.

He also remembered to add a year to his age, too. In China everyone becomes one year older on New Year's Day.

Then Norman started out to visit his friends. Every place he looked he saw red decorations. In China red is the color of good luck.

Norman's pockets were stuffed with presents for his friends. He took lucky red apples and candy. For the children he had red envelopes with a little money in each one. *Gung hay fat choy,* Norman called out to everyone he saw.

In the afternoon the lion dancers came. They roared and jumped and spun and pounced. Up and down the street they danced, chasing away the evil spirits.

As the dancers came to each store, the store owner lit firecrackers. The loud noise would help the lion dancers scare the spirits away. Everyone cheered and clapped. Then the owner put a little money in the lion's mouth to say thank you for the dance.

23

Now it was time for the Dragon Parade. Up and down the main street of Chinatown people waited for the dragon. Where is it? When will it come? people asked.

Suddenly, there it was! Like a great red and gold and green serpent, the dragon danced and pranced along the street. Its bright, fiery eyes flashed wildly. The dragon had a red tongue and many feelers on its head.

Norman knew that this wasn't a real dragon. He could see the thirty men who carried its long silk body. Even so, it was an amazing sight.

25

This was the first Dragon Parade many of the people visiting Chinatown had ever seen. Norman and his friends told them about the dragon. It was made in China, they said, and brought to America on a ship.

They explained that dragons are special animals. Chinese people believe that dragons are strong and good. Once a year, the dragon comes to wish everyone peace and good luck.

When the dragon passed, the parade was over. Now I will wish you a Happy New Year at my house, Norman said. And people headed to Norman's home for the banquet. They were very hungry after such an exciting day.

Everyone looked forward to the big feast at Norman's house. They were not disappointed. Plate after plate of steaming food came out of Norman's kitchen. Soon the banquet table was piled high with fish, chicken, pork, beef, vegetables, and noodles.

Each dish has a special New Year's meaning, Norman told them. The whole fried chicken will bring good luck. The fish will bring enough food and money for the whole year.

Norman and his Chinatown neighbors told the people of San Francisco all about their celebration. They were glad to share their New Year with their new friends.

29

恭喜發財

At the end of the party, Norman stood to speak. Our calendar, he told his guests, follows the moon. Each month begins when there is a new moon in the sky. Every twelve months there is a new year. Each year is named for one of twelve animals—rat, ox, tiger, rabbit, dragon, snake, horse, ram, monkey, rooster, dog, or pig.

Norman raised his glass. He made a toast to the Year of the Ox.

Gung hay fat choy, Norman and his friends said. We wish you good fortune and happiness.

Thank you, thank you, the guests answered. Happy New Year to you.

This was the first Dragon Parade celebrated in the Land of the Golden Mountain. It was a new beginning for everyone.

About the Lunar New Year

Chinese people first came to the United States, the Land of the Golden Mountain, more than 150 years ago. In all of those years they have never missed a Lunar New Year's celebration.

The first Lunar New Year's celebration was small, but as more Chinese arrived in the early 1850s, the festival grew larger. Norman Ah Sing organized the first big celebration, with its Dragon Parade, in 1851.

The Lunar New Year is still the most important festival of the Chinese calendar. It is a time when Chinese-American families come together with the hope of bringing good luck to the family for the new year.

Today more than 100,000 people celebrate the Lunar New Year in San Francisco every year. It is the largest New Year's parade outside of Asia. And like Norman Ah Sing's Dragon Parade, it is a celebration for everyone.